LAYMEN, PROCLAIM THE WORD!

LAYMEN, PROCLAIM THE WORD!

JOSEPH M. STAUDACHER
Professor of Speech, Marquette University

What I tell you in darkness, speak in the light.
What you hear in private, PROCLAIM from the housetops.
— MATTHEW 10:27

FRANCISCAN HERALD PRESS

Library of Congress Cataloging in Publication Data:
Laymen, Proclaim the Word!, by Joseph M. Staudacher.
1. Lay readers.   I. Title.
BX1915.S8   808.5   73-630
ISBN 0-8199-0451-1
Copyright © 1973 by Franciscan Herald Press,
1434 West 51st Street, Chicago, Illinois 60609
MADE IN THE UNITED STATES OF AMERICA

‡‡

NIHIL OBSTAT:
  Marion A. Habig O.F.M.
  Censor Deputatus

IMPRIMATUR:
  Msgr. Richard A. Rosemeyer, J.C.D.
  Vicar General, Archdiocese of Chicago

February 9, 1973

Dedicated to my wife
Rose
who believes in the
Word of the Lord

ACKNOWLEDGMENTS

I wish to thank those who gave special help: Father Mark Hegener O.F.M., Robert Broderick, Gerald Schaefer, Father Carl Last, Father Thomas Caldwell S.J., Burton Boettcher, the many authors listed in the bibliography, and the many priests who gave generously of their time in telephone interviews. Many thanks, too, to Terry Bajczyk who typed the final manuscript.

CONTENTS

INTRODUCTION

WHEN Vatican Council II called upon laymen to participate more fully in the liturgy, one of the more significant areas of service was designated for lectors and commentators. As the form of the liturgy became more developed, this service took on a greater dimension.

Today in churches around the world, men and women are responding to this participation. The role of the lector, who reads the Word of God to the congregation or to the assembly of the faithful, is of the first importance. The same is true of the commentator who assists in a special manner as a leader of singing, the declarer of the liturgy, and as the voice expressing the petitions of the faithful.

Because these were new services in the public worship of the Church, there was a need to train more men and women to make their assistance more devout and effective. Now every church, parish, and chapel needs trained personnel to fulfill these services.

It is to this end that we have prepared and offer this book. Our intent was not to provide an extended course in public performance, but rather to offer a handbook of preparation, an easy directive which would assure the finest performance of service in these roles of active participation in the liturgy. It was also our purpose to give confidence and an implied appreciation to all those who voluntarily assumed these services. We know that in depth of spiritual understanding and the reward of grace from a most bountiful God, the individuals will benefit and in turn reap blessings which each will experience in his own way.

With this lively hope this book is addressed to all who share in the intimate action of the liturgy. May each become in turn more worthy to serve, more dedicated to his participation, and more eager to seek and find the blessings which flow from the Eucharistic celebrations.

J. M. S.

LAYMEN, PROCLAIM THE WORD!

Chapter 1

LAYMEN IN THE LITURGY

SINCE Vatican II laymen and laywomen have been encouraged to take a more active role in diocesan and parish life. They serve on school boards, instructional committees, parish councils and liturgical commissions. Within the liturgy they proclaim as lectors and announce as commentators.

The lay lector and commentator are of recent vintage. Little time has elapsed for the development of a set tradition. Although the pioneers of this movement have earned generous praise for what they have accomplished, it must be evident to even the casual observer and listener that a more professional technique can be developed by many lectors and commentators to insure a fuller and richer lay participation in the celebration of the liturgy.

A few years ago a survey was conducted by the Oakland Liturgical Commission to determine the effectiveness of lectors and commentators. The following percentages emerged:

1. The performer's audibility, his volume, projection, enunciation
    a. effectiveness 60%
    b. ineffectiveness 40%
2. The performer's ability to proclaim, interpret, his impact on the congregation as evidenced by preparation and rehearsal:
    a. effectiveness 20%
    b. ineffectiveness 80%

These percentages are averages and cannot be applied to every reader and to all parishes, but the overall conclusion is clear.

3

There is work to be done.

The writer interviewed at random some fifty priests in a Mid-Western diocese and listened to some well-merited praise for what many of the performers are doing, but in general most of the priests' comments pointed up the following problems:

1. A lack of knowledge of Scripture;
2. The need for voice and diction training, successful experiences and the building of self-confidence;
3. Not knowing what effective reading consists of;
4. Not enough preparation and rehearsal;
5. A failure to realize the important role of the reader of the liturgy;
6. Reading words, not the meaning;
7. The need to get the nose out of the book, to project, enunciate, proclaim and interpret;
8. Too mechanical. Failure to get the words off the paper and into the listener's ears and hearts;
9. Afraid of emotion;
10. Fear of making a mistake, stumbling or mispronouncing a word.

Definitions and Duties

Lectors and commentators can best be defined in terms of their duties. While it is true that frequently one person acts as both lector and commentator and while it is also true that the division of duties between lector and commentator vary from one locality to another, the following analysis is most generally suggested and followed where two laymen participate:

LECTOR

1. Proclaims the Old Testament reading and the Epistle
2. Leads the petitions

COMMENTATOR

1. Does everything else assigned to the laymen from announcing the entrance song to the recessional hymn.
2. In place of a musical director, he sometimes leads the hymns.

Titles

There is some confusion over the terminology used in designating the lector and commentator. Sometimes lectors are called commentators and sometimes both lectors and commentators are called readers or in some instances cantors because they lead the singing. The fact is that none of these words designates accurately either person in terms of his duties. The word "reader" is simply a translation of the Latin word "lector." In addition, the words lector and reader are not accurate in describing the performer's function because he is much more than a reader. He is an oral interpreter of literature, a proclaimer of sacred scripture. As far as the word commentator is concerned, that, too, is inaccurate. A commentator is one who says something "about" something, and yet frequently during the liturgy the commentator is not saying something "about" something. He is merely saying something. While the titles are not rigid, yet they reflect the function of the lay people who speak before the parishioners, lead them in prayer and pray with them. The titles, lector and commentator, have been widely accepted, and we will use these titles in speaking of the various activities of these lay people. Perhaps in time the terms may be changed to accommodate new developments, but for the present we use them although the activities of the lector are those of a "proclaimer" and the commentator is more of an "announcer."

Specific Duties

The specific duties of the lector and commentator are the following:

A. *The Lector*
1. Carries the book in the entrance procession, holding it as an object of dignity. His place in the procession is in front of the celebrant and behind the servers. When the procession reaches the altar, the proclaimer places the book on the ambo (Lectern) and goes to his place.
2. After the collect, he goes to the ambo to proclaim the Old Testament reading, introducing it: "A reading from the Book of . . . . (or Prophet)" . . . . He does not give the chapters, verses or what Sunday it is.

5

After the reading, he pauses, and then says, "This is the Word of the Lord," and returns to his place.

3. After the responsorial psalm the lector again goes to the ambo where he proclaims from the writings of the Apostles, saying: "A reading from the Epistle of the Apostle . . . . to the . . . ." He then repeats at the end: "This is the Word of the Lord," and returns to his place.

4. After the profession of faith when the celebrant has finished introducing the general intercessions of the Prayer of the Faithful, the lector goes to the ambo to lead the petitions. At the end of the petitions he asks the congregation for silent reflection on their needs on a private intention and returns to his place.

B. *Commentator*

1. When all is ready before the celebration of the Eucharist begins, he goes to his place before a microphone (not the ambo) and announces briefly the theme of the liturgy of the day and the entrance song, asking the people to stand.

2. After the first reading he goes to his stand and leads the responsorial psalm.

3. Immediately after the general intercessions, he announces the Offertory Song.

4. During the priests' Communion he announces the Communion hymn.

5. He makes the parish announcements after the pause for thanksgiving and communion prayer.

6. He announces the closing hymn.

7. In general, he keeps all commentary brief, selecting it from a reputable source. Commentary on the theme of the Mass should be made before the entrance hymn and may be made briefly before each reading. Directions for standing, sitting and kneeling should be given to the congregation, as one priest said, in a kind of off hand manner as though they know what to do, and by now most of them do.

This preceding list of duties is not complete, but may vary according to locality. The writer has attempted to simplify and generalize the more common assignments given to both the lector and the commentator. Custom in the parish may cause changes in the activities of either.

One comment might be made on the reading of the petitions by the lector. Is not this function more in line with the duties of the commentator? The lector would then be purely a proclaimer of Scripture.

It should be noted that variations of duties are abundant in many parishes. For just one example, in some churches the organist or choir director announces the hymns and leads the singing and another person performs all other oral work assigned to the lector and commentator.

It is not the purpose of this book to unify details. Let that be the function of the diocesan liturgical commission or, in some cases, of the parish liturgical committee itself under the direction of the pastor.

One conclusion is certain at this writing. Few parishes do everything alike even in one city. And if one travels across the country, he becomes aware of even more variations. No one, of course, should get lost in detail. The larger purposes of lay proclamation and participation should prevail. And now the job at hand is *how* to make that proclamation and participation most efficient.

A Theological Basis

Years ago, a young actor was cast in the role of Shylock in the Merchant of Venice. After several rehearsals he said to one of his fellow actors, "Neither this play nor this part sends me into ecstasy." His fellow actor replied, "Do you think Orson Welles, Lawrence Olivier, George Arliss and other great actors felt that way when they played the part"?

The same comparison might be made with the Sunday readings. Sometimes the performer sounds as though the reading is not sending him into ecstasy, either. The question is, Did the great saints of the past feel that way when they proclaimed the very same lines? It might be inspiring to any proclaimer of scripture to try to imagine how one of his favorite saints might have spoken those lines.

Scripture

Scripture is the greatest script ever written, greater than Sophocles or Dante, Shakespeare or Wilder, because it deals with God's love for man in the pre-Christian times and as expressed in His Son The Eternal Word. Scripture is forever old and time tested, because it deals with man's basic problems, and forever new and provacative for the same reason. As literature it is classic, and to book dealers a delight, for the Bible is the best seller of all time.

Reading scripture aloud, therefore, is not reading a paragraph from an old volume. It is not similar to reading an announcement of a future parish meeting. It is proclaiming the Word of God Who is Christ.

The performer will proclaim Scripture the way he conceives it. If to him the readings assigned are merely ancient words which few understand or listen to, then his presentation will lack motivation, desire, enthusiasm and convincing proclamation. If, on the other hand, he is vividly aware that he is proclaiming Christ, the way, the truth, and the life, then he will perform as though he were showing the people of God the way, giving them the truth from the source of all life, Jesus Christ.

A Lector is a person bubbling with faith. He sees Christ not as someone who *was* but as Someone Who *is* . . . human, divine, community-minded . . . loving and forgiving in the celebration of the Eucharist.

The Proclamation

The layman, as an oral performer of Scripture, is an assistant to the celebrant or priest in his proclamation of the Word of God. He helps the congregation participate more joyfully in the celebration of the Eucharist so that they may radiate love into the lives of others.

While the following question may be largely academic, let us raise it just the same. Which of the following is most important? The listeners, the lector or the scriptural message? From one point of view we can say that since Scripture is the Word of God, it therefore is most important. On the other hand, revelation does not become actualized until it is proclaimed. The Word of God becomes actualized and fully functional in terms of God's creation of man when the Word is proclaimed, and when man responds to that Word. The Word of God in a vacuum is not the Word of God. The Word presumes communication. Man is the object of that Word.

Since the lector is the bridge between the message and the man, the lector becomes essential to the total process in his service, and a kind of trinity of equality is born as the *lector* communicates God's *Word* to His *people*.

The Celebration of the Eucharist

The Eucharist is more than Christ's death and our worship. It is more than a re-enactment. It is a continuation of the Old Testament promises of a Redeemer and the fulfillment of that Redemption culminating in the Resurrection, Ascension and Pentecost. It is a Eucharistic banquet in which we celebrate Christ's presence in the Word of God and in the Bread and Wine. The Eucharist is the offering of that Bread and Wine to the Father in the love of the Holy Spirit. It is the offering of the total Christ, His Humanity, Divinity, and Mystical Body, our very selves to God the Father. The Eucharistic sacrifice is the celebration of the redemption of all of us in Christ.

And finally the Eucharistic celebration is like a mosaic of many patterns and pieces. If the lector is a mere reader, if he is dull and colorless, the mosaic suffers. On the other hand, if he is motivated to perform in the brilliance of his true function, then the Liturgy of the Word becomes a giant, revolving, multi-cut diamond, and the ability of the lector sends light to those who have come to seek hope and reassurance through the Eucharistic sacrifice in the congregation of many and in the Mystical Unity of Christ.

9

Chapter 2

BARRIERS AND THERAPIES

FOR the past several years the writer has gone to many parishes to conduct drill sessions with the lectors and/or commentators. A question often asked is, "How do I get rid of my butterflies?" There are a number of ways. Let's examine them one by one.

1. *Anxiety is normal.* You're not alone. Recognize and accept the fact that almost everyone experiences some anxiety before and during a public performance, especially the first few minutes. This anxiety is revealed in various ways: a feverish feeling, a rapid heart beat, dizziness, difficulty in breathing, a dry mouth, sweaty palms and forehead, nausea, vomiting, diarrhea, knees knocking, general body tremors and many similar and related phenomena. As a result of these subjective reactions, frequently more noticeable to the speaker than the congregation, the performer may reveal the more obvious signs of fear: staring, wandering eyes, weak trembling voice, vocalized pauses, tense or slovenly posture, leaning, swaying, rocking, and sometimes even laughing or crying. These disturbances are not limited to amateurs. Even the professionals confess similar reactions. The celebrated Metropolitan opera star Lily Pons once confessed she was "sick to her stomach" for several hours before every concert performance. Broadway stars have reported the feeling of a wild caged animal, and have sought release in heightened conversation, physical exercise, silence and prayer. The important fact to remember is this: you're not alone.

2. *Rehearse.* Lincoln once observed, "I believe that I shall never be old enough to speak without embarrassment when I have nothing to say." The lector and commentator could translate that quotation into "I believe I shall never be ready to perform without embarrassment when I have failed to rehearse my material." It follows as night the day that the better prepared and rehearsed the performer is, the greater are his chances for decreasing nervousness, apprehension and anxiety, and conversely for increasing self-assurance and self-confidence. The more prepared, the less nervous. The more nervous, the greater need to prepare.

3. *Analyze the situation*: Analyze why you are afraid. An emotion tends to fade away and lose much of its impact when taken apart and analyzed. Why are you afraid? Is the situation strange because you stand there facing "all those people," some of whom are your friends and family? Are you wondering what the priest is going to think while you perform? Remember those closest to you are least critical while the others are least interested in your feelings.

4. *Not all fear is bad.* Recognize the fact that some fear, anxiety and tension are good. They motivate you to prepare and rehearse well, and help you proclaim with charged batteries. The following story is told about John Barrymore one of the greatest of American actors.

Whenever John Barrymore had to face an opening night audience, his hands would begin to tremble, and the butterflies in his stomach would flutter their wings furiously. It was a nerve-shattering ordeal, but one which he understood and expected. It pulled the strings tighter, and kept his performance at a high pitch.

One opening night shortly before the curtain was to go up, the customary panic was missing. His hands were steady, the butterflies were in repose, he was calm and confident. He was so calm and confident that it scared him. His hands began to shake, the butterflies took wing and suddenly everything was back to normal. And he went out on stage and gave a performance worthy of his talent. John Barrymore found out that night what any performer finally learns. Not all fear is bad, because frequently it sharpens your ability to act and react.

5. *See your listeners as they are.* Despite the fact that you may think the biggest problem in performing is self-confidence, the first and most important problem is listener apathy. Most audiences are not critical on the one hand or friendly on the other. Most audiences are passive, indifferent and pre-occupied with their own problems. Social psychologists point out that most audiences are only half attentive, less intelligent than the members would be as individuals, less critical, of lowered responsibility and of increased uniformity.

True, members of an audience may look at a speaker, and appear to be listening, but the fact is that much of the time their thoughts are miles away. What appears to be listening is merely role-playing. As a performer, do not be misled by this make-believe attention. Many of the members of your audience are only making believe that they are giving you their full and undivided attention. Inadvertently they may be hearing sound, but they are not listening. Hearing is getting sound. Listening is getting meaning from sound. If one of the studies made on listening is reliable, you will find that only about twenty-five percent of your listeners will have gotten the central idea of your reading. What you will find about lesser ideas may amaze you.

Since listeners are generally apathetic, you as a performer must take the view that the prime responsibility is on you. It is your job to be well informed, to be rehearsed, to be animated and enthusiastic, to use vocal dramatization and some visual showmanship.

If you take the erroneous attitude that your content is good in itself and that you need not exert yourself in presenting it, then you are not facing the reality of audiences as they are. Remember, you reap what you sow. Your listeners will be as attentive as you cause them to be.

The problems of getting and holding attention are caused by external and internal factors.

The external factors in a church are sometimes inferior

sound systems, poor acoustics, late-comers, loud coughers, crying babies, misbehaving children and even traffic noises outside the church.

Stronger than the external stimuli which compete with getting and holding attention, however, are the internal stimuli inside the head and heart of the listener. Personal problems compete in a thousand variations. Think of the thoughts and emotinos that were running through your mind the last time you listened as a member of an audience. Remember the stimuli within you which offered competition to the performer. Multiply them by the number of persons in the audience. Now you have some idea of what every performer has to compete with.

Getting and holding attention, therefore, is a very real problem, stronger and bigger than the speaker's stage fright. The listeners are so preoccupied with their own thoughts that in many cases they aren't aware of the speaker's nervousness and stage-fright.

6. *Get up and perform.* If you are afraid to perform, it may be because the situation has a certain mystery about it. By getting up to perform you make the mystery disappear and become commonplace. By getting up to perform, you follow Ralph Waldo Emerson's sage advice concerning self-conquest: "Do the thing you fear to do and the death of fear is certain." Do the thing you fear to do. Get up and perform. Follow the method of George Bernard Shaw who when asked how he became an effective speaker said, "I did it the same way I learned to skate . . . by making a fool of myself until I got used to it." Somewhat differently Shakespeare expressed the same thought: "Our doubts are traitors and make us lose the good we oft might win - - - by fearing to attempt." If the situation seems strange therefore, get up, perform and make the unknown familiar.

7. *Build successful experiences.* Get up before your audience with a strong desire to get your ideas across. Do not think of yourself. Think of what you are reading, interpreting or proclaiming, and the effect it could have on your listen-

ers. Think positively. Concentrate on your contribution to the liturgy. Enjoy what you are doing, and let each experience build to a higher level of skill and perfection. Like what you are doing, and love your listeners. Perfect love casts out fear.

8. *Have someone check up.* Occasionally you will want someone to listen to you and to give you constructive criticism. This evaluation should not be purely negative. It should, first of all, point out what you are doing well and only then suggest ways in which you can improve. By working on one weaker point at a time, you will finally achieve the best level of your talent and ability.

In summary, recall that anxiety is normal and that rehearsal and practice promote confidence. Negative emotions dwindle when they are analyzed. Fear can motivate you to do well. See your listeners as they are with their own problems. Perform frequently and build up a series of successful experiences. Have someone verify your progress by having him listen to you and offer helpful suggestions for improvement.

Chapter 3

ORAL INTERPRETATION OF LITERATURE

A Brief History

Oral interpretation of literature has deep roots. For one thing, it preceded *written* literature. For another, the first literature, being poetic in the form of early epics, was recited by one or more voices in various combinations: solo, unison, refrain or antiphonal. Insofar as our study of the lector is concerned, it is interesting to learn that the earliest forms of Scripture were handed down by recitation and word of mouth. The art of reciting aloud is the oldest of all the speech arts.

In the Old Testament the priests and Levites read the Law aloud in the temple, and the psalms were songs that everyone chanted. After the reform by the Pharisees, the synagogues were set up locally (there was only one temple) and laymen were permitted to read Scripture. Visitors were also encouraged to read and to comment.

St. Luke tells us that when Jesus was in Nazareth he went to the synagogue according to his custom and read a portion from Isaiah. In the Acts of the Apostles we read that Paul read from the Scriptures and reasoned with his listeners.

In nearby Greece we are told in the Odyssey by Homer himself of the oral recitation by the minstrel.

In fact, the concept of oral communication of literature became so elevated in classical Greece that only the rhapsodist, a professional reciter of epic poems, was permitted by law to recite Homer. Oral reading of the classics was considered so elegant an art form that Alexander the Great, a student of Aristotle, entertained his guests with classical readings.

Laymen, Proclaim the Word!

In ancient Rome Vergil, Horace and Ovid emerged as the top stars of their era, reading their own poetry before large groups. Recitals became popular in crowded halls. Statius, a great favorite, is described as one having a beautiful voice and a kindly manner.

In the medieval period, because there was as yet no printing press, the great need existed to read the Scriptures to the masses. St. Anthony, St. Basil, St. Jerome and St. Athanasius all testified to the power of the oral recitation of Scripture. St. Augustine urged all readers to develop good voices and clear diction. He agreed with the Greeks that *a word is not a word until it is spoken.* St. Benedict later declared that not only was oral reading most useful but, to be effective, it had to be studied; skills had to be developed, and each selection needed specific rehearsal. As a result, the Benedictine rule influenced oral reading for centuries. In 747 the Council of Cloves elevated oral reading of the Scriptures to the level of a sacred art, suggesting strongly that those who read the Scriptures aloud, read them well.

Down throughout the Renaissance, oral readers became particularly aware of a beautiful voice and articulate diction projected through an artistic style. Many lay readers outside the church read more interestingly than the clergy, and the faithful became impatient with the overly reserved style of the churchmen.

By the eighteenth century oral reading skills began to go in two differing directions. Outside the church, a method of theatrical imitation developed while inside the church a more subdued method of oral reading prevailed. Both styles had their followers.

The nineteenth century began to look at oral reading and techniques for improving it from a scientific viewpoint, and laid the foundations for two counter-balancing principles which Lew Sarett would clarify and popularize in the twentieth century:

1. Effective oral reading uses the techniques of body and voice to bring attention to a high peak . . . BUT DOES SO . . .

2. In a manner that is disarming in its seeming artlessness, its ease and simplicity.

We can conclude that oral reading has deep roots growing out of man's love for beauty and truth, that it is most natural for man to desire to communicate to his fellow man and that communication is most effective when it is based on sound technique and good art.

Definition

Oral interpretation is the art of evoking listener response to an author's work through visual, vocal and verbal communication.

1. *An art* is a skill governed by principles of beauty, imagination and good taste. A work of art should have unity, and all of the parts should be in harmony with that unity. To avoid monotony, a work of art should have variety. All variety and contrast should be guided by the principles of unity and harmony. In addition, nothing should be out of proportion. Everything should be in balance. If anything gets out of harmony the effect is weakened. Finally the whole work of art should have movement which builds with subtlety and gets to its goal, the evocation of response.

2. *Evoking response* is the purpose of oral reading. If there is no listener response, the cycle is incomplete and imperfect. Earlier in these pages we considered the trinity of equality: the lector, the message and the listener. God has done his part with the script, now let the lector and listener do theirs. And for all practical purposes, let the lector take the view that if he does his part well, the chances are that the listener will respond and do his.

3. *An author's work* may be analyzed for three kinds of content: the *intellectual* content of concepts, judgments and reasoning, the *emotional* content of moods and feelings and finally for *beauty* as expressed in the *style* of language.

4. Visual Communication in oral interpretation is more reserved than it is in speaking but, nevertheless, it is there in muscle tone and subtle bodily expression.

5. Vocal Communication is abundant in oral interpretation, and the effective reader learns the techniques of voice and diction.

19

6. Verbal Communication gets down to the author's meaning and why he selected the words he did to convey that meaning.

Interpretation and Speaking

The difference between oral interpretation and public speaking is simple: oral interpretation is delivering someone else's material whereas public speaking is delivering one's own material.

In delivering someone else's material, the lector should pretend "in a way" that he is the author and suggest that he is giving his *own* material. In this way, his performance may sound more believable. While the oral reader is not an actor, he is an actor to some extent. Acting is making believe. Good acting is making believeable. In a sense, therefore, the oral reader is making believe, and the good oral reader is making believeable.

By pretending "in a way" that he is the author, the lector has a good chance of incorporating the believable elements into his rendition: complete familiarity with his material, a responsive body, physical directness and eye-contact, a conversational melody-pattern in his voice, stressing the right words, suggesting subtle moods, using variety in pace, pausing effectively and pronouncing and enunciating acceptably.

The Bible as Literature

Literature deals with man's basic problems, expresses itself in a beautiful and individual style and lets the reader find identification with his own life.

The Bible can be considered literature of the highest level because it meets all of the standards of great literature. The Bible deals with man's basic problems: life and death, love and hate, hope and despair and every other confrontation which man meets in life. In addition, Scripture is, for the most part, simple and clear, vivid, imaginative, creative and individual. In the opening words of Genesis we read, "In the beginning when God created the heavens and the earth, the earth was a formless wasteland, and darkness covered the abyss while a mighty wind swept over the waters." In the Psalms King David tells us that "though I walk in the valley of the shadow of death, I will fear no evil for you are with me, O Lord!" And Jesus warns the Apostles, "I send you as sheep among wolves. Be therefore as simple as doves and as wise as serpents." Indeed, Scripture is literary in thought and expression and man finds therein identification with his own life.

Kinds of Biblical Literature

Individuality in the Bible is expressed in many kinds of literature: *history* in the books of Kings, the sacrificial and ritual *laws* of Leviticus, the *poetry* of the Psalms, the prophetic and inspirational *oratory* of Isaiah and Jeremiah, the *proverbs* of Wisdom, the *parables* of Jesus, the theological *essays* of Paul, the *imaginative flights* of Revelation.

It follows, therefore, that not all Biblical literature is alike: nor is it all proclaimed alike. An Old Testament narrative is read faster than an abstract theological passage from St. Paul, and one of the Psalms is read with more grandeur than a didactic passage from the Book of Wisdom.

Even though the Lector takes time to analyze the kind of Biblical literature he will communicate, he still runs into problems. Scripture is not always immediately as clear as a newspaper article. Some Scripture needs professional guidance for interpretation.

Study of Scripture

Ideally anyone seeking to make the service of Lector his life-long contribution to lay participation, should read the entire Bible and become familiar with the Old and New Testaments. Before reading each book he should read the explanatory material preceding it. In this way, he is able to study the various writings as to purpose, type, style, original audience and the era in which the author wrote.

While it would be ideal if the Lector could put all of the foregoing suggestions into practice, sometimes, particularly in the beginning, there just isn't time or opportunity for this much background work. What is essential, however, is the study of a commentary on the readings assigned for any particular day. One excellent source for this kind of preparation is *The Sunday Readings,* Cycle A, B and C by Father Kevin O'Sullivan O.F.M.

Meaning and Response

In the oral interpretation of Scripture three kinds of meaning become apparent: the meaning which the sacred writer intended, the meaning which the reader understands and communicates and the meaning which the listener responds to. Perfect meaning takes place when all three of these meanings are the same but this ideal is seldom reached. Sometimes the sacred writer is not immediately clear because of the mysterious nature of his subject matter, the imperfections of language, and his own frailty as a writer. Sometimes the Lector does not fully understand, and even when he does, he sometimes fails to communicate. As a result of these problems, is it any wonder that the listener, beset with his own distractions, gets so little from the readings?

Meaning and response go hand in hand. The word "hot" has little meaning for a child until he burns his hand. Sacred Scripture has little meaning for the listener until his sight, his ears, his mind, heart and nobler emotions respond to the beauty and power and majesty of the Word of God. And it is the job of the Lector to effect this response and make meaning come alive from writer to listener.

First Steps in Analysis

In preparation the lector and commentator should determine the Feast Day and look over the readings assigned to see what theme runs through the liturgy. For example, on the first Sunday of Lent for 1972 the theme was based on the way Adam and Eve were confronted with Satan and lost, and the way Christ was confronted with Satan and won, ultimately redeeming us with his total victory over sin and death.

Read the first reading quietly to see how much of it you can understand. Then read it aloud to yourself to see if more meaning begins to emerge.

A reading from the book of Genesis. 2:7-9, 3:1-7 (22)
The Lord God formed man out of the clay of the ground and blew into his nostrils the breath of life, and so man became a living being.

Then the Lord God planted a garden in Eden, in the east, and he placed there the man whom he had formed. Out of the ground the Lord God made various trees grow that were delightful to look at and good for food, with the tree of life in the middle of the garden and the tree of the knowledge of good and bad.

Now the serpent was the most cunning of all the animals that the Lord God had made.

The serpent asked the woman, "Did God really tell you not to eat from any of the trees in the garden?" The woman answered the serpent: "We may eat of the fruit of the trees in the garden; it is only about the fruit of the tree in the middle of the garden that God said, 'You shall not eat it or even touch it, lest you die.' But the serpent said to the woman: "You certainly will not die!

No, God knows well that the moment you eat of it you will be like gods who know what is good and what is bad." The woman saw that the tree was good for food and pleasing to the eyes, and desirable for gaining wisdom. So she took some of its fruit and ate it; and she also gave some to her husband, who was with her, and he ate it. Then the eyes of both of them were opened, and they realized that they were naked; so they sewed fig leaves together and made loincloths for themselves. — This is the Word of God.
Now read the following commentary from Father O'Sullivan:

Today as we begin the liturgical season of Lent, a period of preparation for the sufferings and death of Christ for us, our first and second readings give us the reason why that suffering and death were necessary. God created man, "male and female he created them" (Gen. 1:27) He gave man powers superior to all the other earthly creatures, and expected of him in return obedience and reverence. Man, because of his pride in the gift given him, refused that obedience — with disastrous results that would have everlasting effects on himself and his descendants, had not the mercy of God intervened.

The commentary continues, analyzing for the reader any words and sentences whose meaning might cause difficulty. And the same procedure is followed for the second and third readings. Certainly after a person has read these authoritative commentaries, he can approach the task of oral proclamation with immeasurably more insight and self-assurance, and the effects will be evident in his work.

Getting the Meaning

Once you have read the scriptural passage over and have read the commentary, you will need to study the passage yourself to determine the author's meaning. John Ruskin offers this advice: "Be sure you go to the author to get *his* meaning, not to find yours, . . . and be sure also, if the author is worth anything, that you will not get at his meaning all at once."

The lector should look for three kinds of content: the intellectual, the emotional and the aesthetic.

1. *The intellectual.* The intellectual content appeals to man's reason. Facts and logical conclusions are the raw material of the mind. They form the base, the bed-rock foundation of meaning.

2. *The emotional.* Man is more than a rational animal. He is an emotional being with the power of laughter and tears. That is why literature is more than a philosophical essay. Literature appeals to the whole man: his mind, his spirit, his heart, and emotions. If the intellectual content can be compared to a skeleton, then the emotional content can be compared to flesh and blood.

3. *The aesthetic.* A literary writer in addition to appealing to man's intelligence and emotions decorates his message with the hues and tints of beautiful language and style. A few examples will illustrate the point: "The Lord God formed man out of the clay of the ground and blew into his nostrils the breath of life" . . . or Isaac's words, "the fragrance of my son is like the fragrance of a field that

the Lord has blessed" . . . or the familiar words of Jesus, "I am the good shepherd; the good shepherd lays down his life for his sheep." Scripture literally abounds with figures of speech, poetic insights, and beautiful allusions in sense and sound.

Once the lector has analyzed the selection intellectually, emotionally and aesthetically, he can use various methods for further analysis, as:

1. *Is the meaning obviously clear?* Is it so clear that everyone would read it in practically the same way? Would the lector read it the same way each time? If this is the case, there isn't too much difficulty. About all the reader needs to do is look at the simple meaning and decide which words he will stress and where he will pause. For example, in the sentences:

THERE WERE *FIVE MEN* IN THE GROUP. *ONE* OF
THE MEN/ WORE GLASSES - - -

we see that there is obviously a simple logical meaning, and this simple logical meaning can be brought out by stressing the italicized words and pausing at the vertical lines for meaningful phrasing. Most readers would interpret the words in the same way.

2. *Is the meaning in doubt?* Are various interpretations possible? In the sentence *"I NEVER SAID HE STOLE YOUR MONEY"* various interpretations are possible mainly because the sentence is taken out of context. There is nothing before or after to give any clues as to how the sentence should be interpreted, and even if there were a context, various interpretations would still be possible. In a case like this a commentary may be helpful. If not, the lector should give what to him is a reasonable interpretation.

3. *Is the meaning cloudy?* Sometimes in St. Paul's epistle a sentence or two will appear which could cause the layman difficulty. Even the commentary may not be perfectly clear. About all the reader can do is read the words aloud, and each listener will receive the meaning in the light of his or her experience in life and spiritual development.

4. *Are shades of meaning possible?* Each time a person interprets a reading aloud, he does so "slightly differently," and this

kind of procedure is good because it lends variety of insight to performance and keeps it from growing stale. The important thing to do is to distinguish between essential meanings and superficial ones. The essential meanings should be given the same way each time.

5. *Are there any emotional spots?* In the Old Testament reading, depicting the fall of Adam and Eve, the serpent said to the woman, "you certainly will not die! No, God knows well that the moment you eat of it you will be like gods . . ." In these words can be heard the voice of the conniving father of all lies, Satan himself. Subtle vocal inflections together with insincere facial communication would characterize the interpretation to bring out the emotional meaning.

6. *Are there any sound or language devices?* Sound devices can be found in alliteration (repetition of consonant sounds), assonance (repetition of vowel sounds), onomatopoeia (words that sound like their meaning; for example, splash, thump, swoop). Language devices become apparent in figures of speech. The more common ones are the simile and the metaphor. A simile is a comparison of one thing with another: "the devil goes about *like* a roaring lion seeking whom he may devour." A metaphor does not compare one thing with another, it identifies one thing with another. Jesus does not say, I am *like* a good shepherd. He says, I *am* the good shepherd. The lector should take advantage of these sounds and language devices in his vocal and visual interpretation.

Analyzing a reading for sound and language devices will help the reader respond more acutely to the beauty of the reading, and contribute to the overall balance of intellectual, emotional and aesthetic communication.

Point of View

Point of view simply means, Who is talking? From whose mouth are the words coming? In the Old Testament reading quoted earlier, concerning the fall of Adam and Eve, there are three points of view: the narrator, the serpent and the woman. Each point of view must be kept vocally and visually separate from the other. The tone of voice for the narrator is quite different from the serpent who in turn is more clever than the naive woman. Never should the tone of voice of one point of view creep over into another, otherwise the subtlety of illusion will be destroyed.

Giving the Meaning

Let us assume that the lector has become familiar with the author and his purpose in writing the particular reading to be communicated to the congregation. Let us further assume that the lector has analyzed the reading for its intellectual, emotional and aesthetic content. He is now ready to apply the basic principles which underlie the art of the oral interpretation of literature.

1. *An effective lector identifies with the author.*

Before the author was able to write down his finished product, he had to observe, select, analyze, organize and develop thought and emotion and express this thought and emotion in beautiful language. He literally had to breathe and live, think and feel his efforts until they became a work of art.

The lector of sacred literature must do the same. He must respond to the writer's thought, feeling and beautiful language until he himself has the same thoughts and feelings the author had and the same appreciation for the beauty of language which the author created and developed. This self identification with the author will help the lector pretend "in a way" that he is the author, saturated with the thought, emotion and beauty and capable of communicating it to others.

2. *An effective lector is an individual person.*

Each person comes from a slightly different background. Even identical twins from the same families, neighborhoods, schools and jobs emerge as individuals. Each lector, therefore even though he tries to identify with the author and his work, interprets sacred literature aloud in his own way, and the difference is good, provided the essential meaning is not distorted. Studies of recordings of great actors such as Maurice Evans, Lawrence Olivier and John Gielgud show individual styles and interpretations of Hamlet's "To be or not to be" soliloquy. Despite their differences, they conform in the essentials and for all practical purposes, have more in common than they have differences.

3. *An effective lector is aware of the meaning while he performs.*

The lector must live each moment of oral communication. The moment of preparation is past, it is true. *Now* is the moment of re-creation, the re-creation of the author's original creation. This re-creation is possible only if the lector projects himself into the literature, lets his imagination and dramatic instinct respond keenly to ideas, feelings, sounds, melody, rhythm and emphasis. To re-create, he must think, imagine, see, feel, hear, smell and taste. As a total person he must respond to a total literary effort.

4. *An effective lector has the desire to communicate meaning to the listener.*

Knowledge and scholarship, while essential and basic, are not enough. Action, communication and listener-response must come into being. The lector must "bubble with faith" even though he may not feel like it. If he is not enthusiastic, he *acts* enthusiastic so he can *be* enthusiastic.

The best kind of motivation comes, of course, from within the lector himself. He asks himself questions as basic as: Who wrote the passage? What was he saying? To whom is he saying it? What did he mean? What does it mean today? How can the message enrich the listener's lives? Answers to these questions should give motivation and desire to the lector. If he still cannot "bubble," he must *act* enthusiastic, hoping that his external physical manifestation will work its way inward. Even though this inner feeling does not develop, the lector should pay no attention to it. Many a great actor has not "felt" like it and yet has given an admirable performance by using an artistic technique which got his inner feelings going.

5. *An effective lector is an artist but never arty.*

In general three kinds of performance are possible: the underdone, the overdone and the "just right." Any performance that is *underdone* fails to take advantage of the author's work, the art of proclaiming, and the human nature of the listener. An author's work is full of ideas, emotion and beautiful language. A lector is a person with intelligence, imagination and appreciation of the beautiful. Listeners have minds and hearts and wills which can be supernaturalized by God's love. If a performance is underdone, the message is weakened by poor proclamation and the listener's response is poor.

A performance that is *overdone* calls more attention to the performance than the message. Listeners are quick to detect the insincerity of the artificial ring in the voice or a pseudo - majestic tone-quality. They instinctively know what they like or dislike even though quite often they may not know why. The performer who fails to take the natural judgment of the congregation into account, and focuses more attention on his pompous technique than on his material and the effect it can have on the listeners, is out of balance in his understanding of values. He is a poor artist.

On the other hand, the "just right" performer is a good artist. He realizes that effective oral reading uses the techniques of body and voice to bring attention to a high peak, but does so in a manner that is disarming in its seeming artlessness, its ease and simplicity. The "just right" performer accepts the old Roman teacher Quintillian's advice that "great art conceals art."

All of the foregoing is not to be interpreted in the light that good oral reading is quite reserved. On the contrary, good oral reading is alive and creative. The oral reader is more than a newscaster who is interested mainly in the logical and intellectual content of his material.

The lector is interested in the logical and intellectual content to be sure, but, in addition to that he is inspired by the emotional and aesthetic content. And, above all, he is further inspired by the Word of God and the role he plays in proclaiming that Word as he brings the literature of Sacred Scripture to the people of God.

In summary we should remember that the oral interpretation of Scripture is an art. Its purpose is to evoke response from the congregation. The lector must identify with the author and his work, and communicate the author's work through visual, vocal and verbal communication. Verbal communication is intellectual, emotional and aesthetic.

Chapter 4

VISUAL COMMUNICATION

THE lector communicates with more than words and tone of voice. He communicates visually as well.

What is visual communication? Anything the observer sees: general appearance, stature, girth, weight, looks, dress, hair style, muscle tone, posture, movement, gesture and even the blink of an eye. While it is true that a person cannot do much about his physical being, it is also true that he can do much to improve his appearance and the manner in which his physical being functions.

Appearance

The general rule for the layman's attire is shirt, jacket and tie. Sometimes the parish offers a standard coat or jacket. In the case of women, lectors or commentators, a choir robe would be in order. Sisters, who appear in their habit, would not wear the robe.

Overly long hair on men or women should be controlled. If the lector pushes his hair out of his face any number of times while performing, he distracts his viewers because he splits attention. Each time the viewer watches the performer push back his hair, he loses part of the message.

Dress should be in good taste and should not draw undue attention. Noisy jewelry on women should be avoided.

Bodily Action

Whether one is reading his *own* material or performing the material of others, he communicates simultaneously in three ways: visually, vocally and verbally.

When someone is speaking his own material, we tend to believe first what we see, especially the facial muscle movements and arm or hand gestures. Secondly, we tend to believe what we hear in the "tone of voice" and finally we believe the words themselves.

When someone is performing the material of *others* for us, we are much more impressed by that material if the body and voice of the performer respond interestingly and believably to the material.

The differences between the delivery of a speaker giving his own material and a reader giving someone else's material are these: (1) A speaker, someone giving his own material, uses more bodily action, showmanship and dramatization than the reader. (2) A reader's vocal effort will be more dramatic, subtle, and artistic than the speaker because the finished script is there in all of its polished literary perfection.

How much bodily action does a lector use? The answer to this question is found in distinguishing between *OVERT* (obvious) and *COVERT* (subtle) bodily movement. Overt action is conspicuous and easily discernible action such as big open gestures. Covert action is more subtle, revealed in highly restrained muscle movements as smiling or frowning. When reading the liturgy aloud, the lector uses very little overt bodily action since his concentration is on the printed page. This concentration, however, should not keep his body from being responsive. His bodily response, while primarily covert, should suggest a tone and an attitude high in personal interest with a strong desire to communicate. Bodily action should be revealed, but in a reserved manner.

Definition

What is bodily action? Bodily action is visual communication in the form of bodily language or bodily expression. Examples of *bodily language* are the finger signs used in the manual alphabet of the deaf, the arm signs used with flags in semaphore signaling, the bodily signs and pantomime of referees and umpires. These visual indications are set, pre-determined procedures, and all persons using them are expected to make them alike. Examples of *bodily expression* are the excited manifestations of children at play, the enthusiastic physical demonstrations of spectators at an athletic contest or the irate gesticulations of someone in an argument. These visual indications are individual and spontaneous. They are the personalized expression of thought and emotion.

The basic difference, therefore, between bodily language and bodily expression is this: bodily language is mechanical and built up from the outside-in whereas bodily expression is motivated and generated from the inside-out.

Bodily Action For the Lector

Ideal bodily action for proclamation of the scriptures should spring mainly from the inside-out with occasional modifications for the outside-in. The performer should concentrate mainly on *what* he is reading, and yet he should give some thought to *how he* is reading. He cannot do merely what comes naturally or he may engage in mannerisms unacceptable to his viewers. On the other hand, if he gives too much attention to how he is performing, he may develop an undue concern for the mechanics of reading and make his listeners more aware of his technique and less attentive to his material. In general, if the lector or commentator has an eagerness to share his ideas with his listeners, if he is animated and enthusiastic, and if he strengthens his desire to communicate, his bodily action will be effective unless he makes specific violations in these areas: walking, sitting, posture, gesture, facial expression and eye-contact.

1. *Walking.* A reading begins before the first word is spoken. A lector tells the congregation something about himself by the way he walks in the procession and to the ambo. He reveals his state of mind. The lector should walk crisply with self-assurance and should suggest a positive attitude. He should avoid walking as though on eggs, lumbering, plodding or any movement that suggests the insecurity of exhibitionism. His bearing should suggest a good emotional state.

2. *Sitting.* Be comfortable without slouching, and alert without being rigid.

3. *Posture.* An overly formalized posture suggesting the orator in practiced delivery is not the best criterion. Equally bad are

leaning, swaying, foot-shifting, pushing back overly long hair and similar, distracting mannerisms. Good posture is a balanced blend of ease and strength. Be comfortable but look alive.

4. *Gesture.* A gesture is more than the movement of a hand. A gesture can involve the whole body or a part of it. For convenience of study we say there are four kinds of gesture: the locative by which someone points, for example, to which way is north; the descriptive, by which the size of a box is indicated; the emphatic by which a fist is pounded on a table to stress a point; and the suggestive, by which someone tries to indicate the immensity of the universe. With the exception of the descriptive gesture for example, indicating the size of a box (which would involve a speaker's hands), all of the other gestures could be made with the speaker's head: pointing north, stressing a point or indicating the immensity of the universe. However weak these examples may be, the principle is clear: a gesture is more than the movement of a hand. The lector however will need few gestures to emphasize his reading.

We can look at gesture from three view-points: the outdated, the unrealistic and the artistic.

Outdated are those manifestations of bodily action which involve too much posing or flamboyance. The performer is too studied, too obvious, too arty. He is more interested in himself and his technique than he is in getting the Word of God into the hearts of his listeners.

The unrealistic way of looking at gesture is based on no bodily response at all. This philosophy confuses extreme reserve with good manners and the lack of physical expression with good art.

Artistic gesture, on the other hand, is balanced and goes to no extremes. It sees man, whether performer or listener, as he is: a bundle of bones, muscles, flesh and blood, nerves, sensations, feelings, emotions and the power of intellect and will. Artistic gesture follows Shakespeare's admonition: "Let your own discretion be your tutor. Suit the action to the word, the word to the action with this special observance that you o'erstep not the modesty of nature."

5. *Facial Expression.* The face, particularly the eyes, can do

much to make the reading vivid. The way to develop an expressive face is not to stand before a mirror and "make faces" but to get so involved with the reading mentally and emotionally that the whole body responds and, with it, the face. Some faces are not interesting because the people behind them are not interested or haven't taken the time to get interested!

6. *Eye-contact.* When to look up from the material may cause some difficulty. First of all, the lector cannot and need not look at the congregation very much. In fact, attempting to look up from the printed page too frequently may do more harm than good. Too much looking up can effect faulty phrasing through loss of place. All the performer needs to do is look up often enough to create the illusion that he is in visual contact with his listeners. When he does look up, he should do so not indiscriminately, but at the ends of thought groups (phrases, clauses, sentences) to keep himself from losing the place and of upsetting the continuity of communication.

Values of Bodily Action

What can bodily action do for the performer? Bodily action relieves nervous tension. Nervous energy comes in through the nerves and goes out through the muscles. If the lector concentrates on what he is saying and lets his body respond to his material, he will experience a lessening of nervousness and a strengthening of confidence. Bodily response helps the performer break through the fear barrier.

Bodily action helps in another way. It stirs up enthusiasm and helps the vocal effort. Once a person begins to *act* animated, he tends to *be* animated. By unlocking his bodily response, the reader unlocks his feeling and thinking. The body and mind are inseparable; they work together.

Empathy

Many of the idioms of our language are expressed in bodily terms:

the cold shoulder	hot under the collar
heart of stone	butterflies in my stomach
on your toes	dollar signs in his eye balls
my knees knocked	little pitchers have big ears

These expressions help us feel in our muscles what the speaker feels in his muscles; and that is what empathy is all about. It is a "feeling in" what the other person is feeling, an imaginary projection of oneself into the consciousness of another human being.

What are the implications of empathy for the lector? To answer that question we need to take, in a nutshell, an overall view of the process of oral interpretation.

A writer has certain experiences. While undergoing these experiences, he senses, feels, has emotional and muscular reactions, thinks, reasons and arrives at conclusions and values. The writer records these experiences in the form of thoughts, emotions and beautiful expression. Inherent in the author's words are those muscular experiences which he himself lived through either really or in imagination.

Now the performer of literature enters the picture. He reads the author's work silently or aloud and experiences very closely those moments which the author experienced. As the performer enters into those experiences imaginatively, something happens to his muscles. He feels the facial expression of the serpent as it communicates lies to the woman. He feels the shame of the man and woman as they stand clothed only in fig leaves.

The next step in the process of oral interpretation is the performer's communication of those muscle movements to the listeners. If the performer identifies himself with the material, if his body responds, if his voice responds, and if the listener feels *IN HIS MUSCLES* what the author felt, then, we say that through *EMPATHY* the communicative process is complete because the listener responds to the performer who responds to the author who responded initially to set the entire process in motion.

In summary, the lector should take appearance into account. He should let his body respond to the author's material in a reserved, artistic, but real and effective manner. The lector should let the bodily response come mainly from the inside-out. Walking, sitting and posture are based on ease and strength. Gesture and facial expression are in response to the material; eye-contact is based on phrasing. Empathy is "feeling in."

Chapter 5

VOICE AND DICTION

TO a large extent the people of God judge the Old Testament readings and the epistles by the way you proclaim them. Your voice and diction, your oral and visual interpretation and speech do much to make Scripture more attractive to others or less so.

Your vocal efforts have the power to make sacred ideas and emotions shine like jewels, or conversely, to reflect communication that is dull, ineffective and even irritating.

Before you can begin to improve your vocal technique and develop higher forms of artistic skills, you should first develop an *awareness* of what is meant by good voice and diction. Secondly, you should develop a *desire* to improve. You proclaim today as you did yesterday, and you will proclaim tomorrow as you do today unless some reason gets in the way to make you change.

What reasons can help you change? Is it love of God's message to man and the part you play in getting that message across? Is it pride in your service before others? Is it the sense of accomplishment that comes from achieving excellence as an artist? Is it the reward that comes from loved ones and friends in their approbation of your efforts? Is it the ring of those centuries-old words of approval, "Well done, good and faithful servant . . ."

Before you can make vocal improvement, you should understand what your specific problems are. You will find them explained under one or more of the following problem areas: environment, personality, anatomy and vocal skills.

Environment. You learned to speak originally by imitating others. Go back in memory a number of years, and recall how your home, neighborhood, school, friends and place of employment shaped your speech.

For example, at home: Jim's father worked in a noisy machine shop. To be heard in the shop, he used a volume level which was good for the shop but excessive when carried over into the home. His children unconsciously imitated him, and talked too loudly. Tom's father was an accountant. Working in a quiet office, he developed a modulated voice. His children imitated. Sally's mother was nervous and excitable. Her voice was high-pitched and tense. Mary's mother was relaxed and jolly. Her voice was musical and emotionally adjusted. Both mothers left their imprint on their families.

Besides the home, other influences are at work. Just as you can recognize speech differences among individuals from different parts of the country, so you can, if you live in a large city, notice speech variations in different neighborhoods, among various associates and in places of employment. These facts point to a significant conclusion: environment affects personality and personality affects voice.

Personality. A voice doesn't talk; a person does, and a person is a combination of his ancestors, his environment, his sense of values and his freedom of choice. You as a lector cannot change your ancestors, but by your freedom of choice you can do much to change your environment and develop what good and thinking men consider a strong sense of values.

"What you are, thunders so loudly I cannot hear what you say," said Emerson. Think about that statement in terms of your voice, and the effect it has on others. The words you utter may say one thing, but the entire vocal effect may suggest meanings you don't intend. Your personality has been at work on your voice.

You reveal your true personality largely through your temperament. Your temperament is your emotional disposition toward a situation. For example, when someone steps on your foot in a crowd do you push forward, fight back, move away or feel sorry for yourself? When you see a bully picking on someone, do you step in between them, fight the bully, walk away, or get disgusted with human nature?

The emotional drives behind your actions are neither bad nor good. Their badness or goodness depends upon the way you use them.

Negative Temperaments. Four persons were walking down a path one day: Mr. Bold, Mr. Bad, Mr. Lazy, and Mr. Sad. In the middle of the path stood a bale of hay. Mr. Bold pushed the others out of the way, and jumped over the bale. Mr. Mad got angry, and kicked it. Mr. Lazy avoiding trouble, walked around it. Mr. Sad, perturbed and melancholy, sat down on it and cried.

How might these individuals reveal their personalities through their voices?

- Would Mr. Bold be too loud? Be an exhibitionist with more concern for manner than communication?
- Would Mr. Mad be throaty, grating, rough and raspy? Would he be over-bearing with a super-abundance of falling inflections?
- And Mr. Lazy. Dull, monotonous, and boring?
- Mr. Sad. Breathy, whiney, nasal?

Positive Temperaments. Four friends were walking down the street one day: Mr. Energetic, Mr. Righteous, Mr. Relaxed, and Mr. Sympathetic. Two cars collided. One of the passengers was thrown to the pavement. Mr. Energetic ran to call the police. Mr. Righteous pursued the guilty driver running away. Mr. Relaxed, took out a notebook and wrote down the facts. Mr. Sympathetic covered up the injured person with his coat.

How might these individuals reveal their personalities through their voices?

- Would Mr. Energetic sound enthusiastic? Would his voice suggest an interest in his message and in others? Would he make a good lector or commentator?
- Would Mr. Righteous make a good crusader? An effective pleader for good causes? Would he make a good lector or commentator?
- Would Mr. Relaxed give evidence of well-adjusted voice

machinery? With mellow, musical sounds? Would he make a good lector or commentator?

- Would Mr. Sympathetic be sensitive to emotional tone-color and vivid words? Be understanding and tolerant? Would he make a good lector or commentator?

The lector and commentator can use all of the foregoing positive personality traits to good advantage, and anything, therefore, that can be done to improve personality will help to improve voice. Remember, an interesting personality will improve your voice for reading aloud.

Anatomy. The physical elements in voice production can be grouped under generator, vibrator, resonator, articulator, and evaluator.

Generator. Observe the sleeping Mr. Smith on an operating table. He lies there breathing easily. Notice the stomach area rising and falling. Notice, too, the rib cage expanding and contracting. This is normal breathing to sustain life.

Apply this observation to your own breathing. Lie down flat on your back. Place a book on the stomach area. Relax and breathe. Notice how the book is elevated and lowered. Feel the rib cage expand and conrtact. This, too, is normal breathing to sustain life.

Now stand up. Relax. Let your arms fall and hang. Inhale just the way you did when you were flat on your back. Notice the stomach area protrude. Feel the rib cage expand. Exhale. Notice the stomach area return to its normal shape. Feel the rib cage contract. Again, this is normal breathing to sustain life.

Breathing for public reading is fundamentally the same with these additions:

In ordinary breathing to sustain life you inhale rather slowly. In breathing for public reading you inhale more quickly and deeply.

In ordinary breathing to sustain life, you exhale rather quickly. In breathing for public reading, you exhale slowly as you control the output of air against the vibrating vocal cords.

In order to improve your breathing-skills for public performance, you should understand how you control the input and output of air in your lungs.

Inside your stomach area is a big muscle called the diaphragm that looks like an upside-down mixing bowl. When you inhale, it tends to flatten out. When you exhale, it returns to its bowl-like shape. If you inhale while you're lying down, it tends to flatten out toward the opposite wall. If you inhale while you're standing, it tends to flatten out toward the floor.

In addition to the action of the diaphragm, the rib muscles are also at work. When you inhale, the rib muscles in the front, sides and back, pull the ribs out. When you exhale, the ribs contract to their original position.

The more the diaphragm pulls down, and the more the rib muscles pull out, the more room there is for the lungs to expand for the in-rushing air. The more slowly the diaphragm and ribs return to their original position, the more efficiently can you control the output of air against the vibrating vocal cords.

Vibrator. Blow up a balloon. Hold the neck of the balloon with the forefinger and thumb of each hand. Now stretch the neck of the balloon horizontally so that the air escapes in a squealing sound. The balloon, of course, represents your lungs; the stretched neck of the balloon, your vocal cords.

Your vocal cords are housed in the larynx, commonly referred to as the Adam's apple. Set in the front of the neck, the larynx is more prominent in men than in women.

The muscles around the vocal cords, unlike the powerful diaphragm and rib muscles, are small and delicate, and can be strained easily by too much tension. They should, therefore, be used in as relaxed a manner as possible. Let only the pitch come from the vocal cords. Let the power come from the diaphragm and the rib muscles.

Resonator. Say, "Boom." Now say it into a metal waste basket. Hear how much fuller the sound is? Something similar happens to the sound vibrated by your vocal cords when it passes into your throat, nose, and mouth. The sound is made bigger, richer, and fuller. The more open your throat is, the less obstructed your nose is, and the more efficiently your mouth is shaped, the more will the vibration of the vocal cords be enlarged into bigger, richer, fuller sounds.

Articulator. Say, "This champion." Now say it again, feeling the movement of your tongue, teeth, lips, lower jaw, and soft palate (roof of your mouth nearest your throat). The efficient use of these articulators is necessary if you want your enunciation to produce full vowel sounds and crisp, clear consonant sounds. Lazy, listless articulators produce enunciation that is muffled, indistinct, and uncommunicative.

Evaluator. Your ear ultimately is your best teacher, because if you can't hear what you are doing, you can't make the right change if you need to. Asking others to listen to you is good, but, ultimately *you* must hear how you are performing if you want to make an adjustment. Learn, therefore, to listen critically to your own performance. In the process be careful not to be so concerned with your voice that you forget the message. Above all, avoid falling in love with the sound of your own voice which invites artificial and affected mannerisms. While you must give *some* conscious effort to *how* you sound, do so mainly during rehearsal. During the actual performance listen to yourself critically as little as is necessary. Concentrate mainly on the meaning of the material during your performance.

Vocal Skills. During rehearsal you listen to your vocal efforts and measure their effectiveness according to the following fundamental vocal skills: force, range, quality, diction, and pacing.

Force. Force is concerned with volume and emphasis.

1. *Volume.* The first vocal rule in public reading is, "Fill the room with your voice." Breathe deeply and fully. Get your voice out on the air. Make it easy for your listeners to hear you. If you feel self-conscious the first few times you hear your voice rolling out with melodious authority, pay no attention to your embarrassment. Concentrate, rather, on your message and your satisfied listeners who hear without strain.

2. *Emphasis.* Emphasis is used to stress certain words and to build to a climax.

    a. *Stress certain words.* Some words are more important

than others. What are they? The meaning you wish to convey will tell you. Read the following sentence seven times. Stress the first word the first time, the second word the second time and so on:

I NEVER SAID HE STOLE YOUR MONEY.

Notice in the following sentence how the word *"one"* must be stressed to bring out the full meaning:

There were *seven men* in the group; only *one* of the men was an *athlete*. If, instead of stressing the word "one" in the second part of the sentence, you stress the word "men," you fail to communicate a fine shade of meaning.

One word of warning. Avoid stressing too many words. All light and no shadow results in no picture.

b. *Build to a climax.* Frequently you as a lector will find that your material builds to a high moment. Take advantage of this situation. Build to a climax. You strengthen meaning and add variety to your delivery. Notice how the following sentence from St. Peter's first epistle builds to a climax:

But you are a chosen race, a royal priesthood, a holy nation, God's own people that you may declare the wonderful deeds of him who called you out of darkness into his marvelous light. (I Peter 2:9)

Range. Range is concerned with pitch, inflection, and melody-pattern.

1. *Pitch.* Your voice is capable of many different pitches. How high you can go or how low depends upon the size and shape of your vocal cords. The longer and thicker your cords are, the lower will be your range; the shorter and thinner your cords, the higher will be your range. Since you cannot change the basic size or shape of the cords, the next best procedure is to learn to use well what you have.

You can learn to pitch your voice properly within your natural range by considering your middle pitch, your best pitch, and your habitual pitch.

Your best pitch, around which you build your rising and falling inflections should be slightly below your middle pitch. This best pitch should become your habitual pitch. If your habitual pitch is too high, however, your upper range will sound strained on a rising inflection and tend to get nasal. If your habitual pitch is too low, your lower range will sound tight on a falling inflection and tend to get throaty or produce a false resonance called "glottal fry."

When reading very loudly to make a point dramatically, do so with increased abdominal force, but do not use the upper range.

When engaging in highly emotional communication, use a more intense quality if proper, but, unless an acting situation demands it, do not use the upper range too much. Too much upper range causes vocal strain.

2. *Inflection.* Inflection, which is a vocal glide on a word or syllable, can be falling, rising, or a combination of the two.

    a. *Falling.* A falling inflection is normally used to make a statement. It suggests confidence, assurance, and authority. Too many falling inflections may suggest an egotistic or overbearing person.

    b. *Rising.* A rising inflection is normally used to ask a question. It suggests doubt, uncertainty, and indecision. Too many rising inflections may suggest a lack of self-confidence.

    c. *Combinations.* These combinations can be two-fold: rising-falling or falling-rising. They can be used effectively to suggest subtle meanings. As techniques, they are helpful in preparing material for oral reading or acting.

        Rising-falling. When Mark Antony in "Julius Caesar" says, "Brutus is an honorable man," something less than *honorable* is detected in the rising-falling inflection.

        Falling-rising. When Shylock in the "Merchant of Venice" says, "Hath a dog money" something more than a *dog* is inferred in the falling-rising inflection.

3. *Melody-pattern.* Melody-pattern is simply a succession and mixture of all kinds of vocal inflection. If the melody-pattern sounds conversational, we say the person is natural. If it doesn't,

we say the person is artificial or mechanical and sounds stilted.

When we talk about someone reading aloud in a "conversational style," we are referring primarily to the melody-pattern in his voice. We assume that he uses the proper amount of volume demanded for public performance. Even before a microphone, more volume is demanded than in ordinary conversation to achieve a well-projected voice.

Quality. The quality, resonance, or timbre of your voice is dependent upon two factors: Your emotional reaction to what you are saying and the way your physical mechanism functions.

1. *Your emotional reaction.* If you are in a good emotional state with a minimum of fear and a maximum of enthusiasm, the emotional quality of your voice will be good. Fear tenses and constricts the muscles, and all the knowledge in the world of vocal anatomy and its operation helps little until you have acquired a reasonable amount of self-confidence through successful experience. A lack of enthusiasm is equally disastrous. A lector without enthusiasm, without motivation, without a desire to communicate is little more than a physical robot. To repeat what was said earlier, a voice doesn't talk; a person does. Therefore, put your whole being into what you are doing, and the emotional quality of your voice will improve.

2. *Your physical mechanism.* Physically you can improve your voice quality by full, deep breathing, a relaxed larynx, an open throat, and front-forward placement.

    a. *Full, deep breathing.* Full, deep breathing is essential to good voice quality. A generous supply of air is necessary to support the tone initiated by the vocal cords. If you want your vocal motor to hum, you've got to give it some gas.

    b. *A relaxed larynx.* Relax your voice box to avoid a pinched tone which may produce hoarseness, but tense your vocal cords sufficiently to produce a pure tone which lends itself to better resonance. Overly relaxed vocal cords permit air to escape into the overall tone which results in a breathy quality.

c. *An open throat.* Yawn. Relax those tensed muscles in your throat. Make room for the vibrations coming from your vocal cords to become bigger, richer, and fuller. Think of your voice as poured from a pitcher, not squirted from a hose.

3. *Front-forward placement.* The only sounds in American speech that should go through the nose are m, n, and ng. Therefore, direct all other sounds out front-forward as though they were hitting just above your upper front teeth. As an experiment, say "Ho." Now say it again, holding your nose shut. If part of the sound is attempting to come through your nose, you have not achieved complete, front-forward placement. Try it again until all of the "O" sound is directed out front-forward.

Diction. While the word diction is used in the field of English composition and literature to designate choice of words, the same word in the field of Speech is used to include distinct enunciation and acceptable pronunciation.

1. *Enunciation.* Enunciation is the manner of articulating vowel and consonant sounds distinctly by means of the tongue, teeth, lips, lower jaw, and soft palate. If your articulators are sluggish, your enunciation will be indistinct. If your articulators are active, your vowel sounds will be full and your consonant sounds, crisp. If your articulators are overly active, your enunciation will be exaggerated.

Some performers look like ventriloquists when they talk. They seldom move their lips. Others speak with such exaggeration, they make their listeners overly aware of their enunciation. Avoid extremes. Let your vowels be full and your consonants crisp but let the process be effortless and easy.

Take the circumstances into account. What may be adequate in a small church may not be sufficient for a larger one with acoustical problems. What may be just right before a public address microphone, may be too enlarged before a lapel microphone held too close to your mouth.

Finally realize that for liturgical performance much of good enunciation is a matter of ear training through trial and error.

You read. Someone listens and tells you he can't understand easily parts of what you are saying. You try again. This time he tells you that your enunciation is better in general but, exaggerated in spots. You make adjustments. After much experience under varying circumstances in different-sized churches you develop skill in producing enunciation that is effortless and efficient for this or that situation. Your ear becomes attuned through trial and error to what is adequate and efficient.

    2. *Pronunciation.* Pronunciation is the expression of sounds and accents of words in connected speech and in conformity with acceptable standards. From this definition, four key ideas arise: sounds, accents, connected speech, and acceptable standards.

      a. *Sounds.* The basic sounds in words are vowels and consonants. Mispronunciations occur when vowels or consonants are added, omitted or substituted.

Words can be mispronounced when sounds are added:
ARTHU*R*ITIS FOR ARTHRITIS
*T*CHICAGO FOR CHICAGO
IDEA*R* OF FOR IDEA OF

Words can be mispronounced when sounds are omitted:
ALUMNUM FOR ALUM*I*NUM
LIB*R*ARY FOR LIB*R*ARY
HONORBUL FOR HONOR*A*BLE

Words can be mispronounced when sounds are substituted:
FEB*Y*UARY FOR FEBRUARY
DEM FOR *TH*EM
LE*N*TH FOR LE*NG*TH (ng is considered one sound)

      b. *Accents.* Accents as used here does not refer to foreign accent but to the stress placed on a syllable. While many words admit of differently accented syllables, some words do not. A word can be mispronounced, therefore, by misplacing the accent:
MYOÓ-ZEE-UM for MYOO-ZEE-UM
DEÉ-TROYT for DEE-TRÓYT
THEE-AY'-TER for THEÉ-UH-TER

c. *Connected speech.* Connected speech refers to the pronunciation of words not as single words, but as used in combination with other words. The word BECAUSE is usually pronounced BEE-CÁWZ as an individual word, but in connected speech, unless the speaker wishes to emphasize BECAUSE, he may correctly pronounce it BEE-CÚZ. The purpose of speech is communication, and not to call undue attention to itself. Readers who pronounce every syllable of every word in connected speech the way they pronounce words singly fail to follow Shakespeare's wise advice:

Speak the speech, I pray you, as I
pronounced it to you, trippingly on
the tongue, but if you *mouth* it as
many of your players do, I had as lief
the town crier spoke my lines.

Connected speech permits no pauses in the sentence, "Pat takes science." Pausing after "Pat" or "takes" would be affected and overdone.

Examples of other pronunciation variations in connected speech involve the simple words A (uh) and THE (thuh).

Don't say, AY MAN. Say UH MAN. Use AY only for emphasis, as, for example, "I didn't ask all of you to help. I asked for AY (one) helper."

Don't say, "THEE MAN." Say, "THUH MAN," or better, "TH'MAN." Say THEE for emphasis, as, for example, "He is THEE man of the hour." Or say THEE BEFORE A VOWEL SOUND, "THEE APPLE" or "THEE F.H.A." Even though F in F.H.A. is called a consonant, it begins with a vowel sound.

A word of warning: in addition to acceptable pronunciation in connected speech, clear enunciation must always prevail. In the following widely different circumstances you will do well to follow these general rules:

Don't overdo your diction before a *broadcast* microphone. You'll sound exaggerated. Don't underplay your diction in public performance before a large gathering or before a *public address* microphone. You must project!

d. *Acceptable standards.* An acceptable standard is a model, agreed upon by experts for imitation. Language experts agree that there is no one pronunciation standard, acceptable for all words in American speech. Generally they recognize three broad areas: Eastern, Southern and General American, and even in these broad areas they recognize acceptable variations.

While it may be emotionally difficult for some persons to be tolerant of pronunciations of different areas, it must be admitted that language is the result of usage and not of preconceived rules. This is not to say that because thousands of persons say toity-toid for thirty-third or dis for this or hep for help that these pronunciations are correct. Each locality has its unacceptable provincialisms. The stress here is on acceptability. But acceptability presupposes some kind of uniformity. Since this uniformity is found more frequently among the better-educated users of language, it follows that if there is any acceptable standard at all, it must be this: SPEAK THE LANGUAGE THE WAY MOST OF THE BETTER-EDUCATED PERSONS IN YOUR GENERAL AREA SPEAK IT.

To determine what pronunciations are used by the better-educated in your general area, listen to clergymen, teachers, political speakers, announcers and other professional persons well-versed in language. Even among these speakers you will hear some variations. Choose those pronunciations for your own that sound most general and least different.

The same applies to the dictionary. When more than one pronunciation is listed, choose the one that sounds most like the one used in your general area.

Pacing. Pacing is the amount of vocal movement in given periods of time. A good reader develops variety in pacing. This skill is achieved through a change in rate, sensitivity to rhythm, and use of pause.

1. *Change in rate.* Rate is the number of words spoken in a given period of time. Rate is determined by your personality, material, listeners, and accoustical situation.

   a. *Your personality.* By nature you may be quick or slow. If you're the race-horse type, you may need to slow down. If your rate is that of the plough-horse, you need a greater zest for communication. Runaway speech leaves listeners behind. Plodding speech puts them to sleep.

   b. *Your material.* You deliver happy and simple material at a faster pace than the dignified or complex, but in either case, to insure variety, look for opportunities to slow down or speed up.

   c. *Your listeners.* How much do they know about your material? What do you want them to get out of it? You read Scripture more slowly to a group of third graders hearing it for the first time than to adults who have heard it often, but even when reading to adults the lector should be careful to read slowly enough for comprehension and articulately enough for understanding.

   d. *The acoustical situation.* The larger the listening area, the more slowly you speak. Typical is the large church built more for majesty and beauty than for good acoustics. The beginning speaker who finds himself in a similar situation almost always talks too fast. All acoustical situations, of course, are not so extreme. Under easier circumstances you use a less deliberate rate. Be sure, however, that you make yourself understood first. Only then should you think about variety in rate.

2. *Sensitivity to rhythm.* Rhythm is the rise and fall of

sound with an overall regularity marked by intermittent variation. Waves washing up on shore afford a good example. Their rise and fall have an overall regularity with intermittent variation. The regularity supplies the unity, and the variation breaks up the possible monotony. Notice the rhythm in the following:

> But Ruth said, Do not ask me to abandon or forsake you. For wherever you go I will go; wherever you lodge, I will lodge; your people shall be my people, and your God my God. Wherever you die, I will die, and there be buried (Ruth 1:16-17).

Rhythm is closely associated with emotion. The execution of rhythmic passages demands a sensitive artist who thinks and feels with the rise and fall of the undulating hills and valleys of the author's emotions.

The way to capture the rhythm of a selection is to read it aloud several times until your ear and your intuition tell you that you have captured the mood, the changes in mood and the corresponding variations in rhythm.

3. *Use of pause.* You pause to breathe, to insure meaning, to promote reflection, and to create a dramatic effect.

    a. *Pausing for breathing.* The confident lector who has developed the habit of filling the room with his voice usually gives little thought to the pauses he takes for breathing. Sometimes, however, in reading aloud, he makes a conscious effort to breathe deeply at certain points to keep from running out of breath at the end of a long passage. Pausing for breath, before completing the passage, weakens the meaning and dramatic effect.

    b. *Pausing for meaning.* The more complicated the meaning, the more are pauses necessary to help the listener understand. Experienced lectors, especially when reading certain passages from St. Paul, use pauses generously to bring out the meaning clearly. They know how helpful these pauses are for listener understanding.

The most effective way to pause for meaning is to break up longer s e n t e n c e s into thought-groups. A thought-group may be a word, a phrase, or a clause.

Sometimes a thought-group can even be several short sentences. For example, "Look out!! The car!! Your baby!!" Any pause between those words might result in tragedy.

All of which leads to an important distinction in reading. Don't be misled by punctuation marks, but be aware of them as aids to clarity. Sometimes you pause at a punctuation mark, and sometimes you don't. The sentences, "Look out!! The car!! should be evidence enough.

c. *Pausing for reflection.* Strongly recommended is a pause at the end of each reading to enable the congregation to reflect on the passages just read. After a pause the lector looks up and out at the congregation, saying, "This is the Word of the Lord," inviting their response, "Thanks be to God."

d. *Pausing for dramatic effect.* There are many ways to highlight an idea or emotion. It can be done by stress, understress, inflection, change in emotional quality, or by pause, before or after the idea or emotion. Notice how in the following examples a dramatic effect is achieved through pause:

So you're a - - - - big shot now!

To be - - - or not to be - - - that is the question.

I don't believe that. Throw it - - - out.

In summary the lector should take inventory of his voice: the influences of his environment, his personality characteristics, understand the nature and operation of his speech anatomy, and the manner in which he uses the functional skills of force, melody quality, diction, and pacing.

Chapter 6

THE PRACTICE SESSION

EXCELLENCE in lectors and commentators, is closely correlated with general educational backgrounds. The higher the educational level, the less direction is needed. Whatever the educational level may be, however, at least some direction is necessary. This direction should be afforded by one of the priests, and under him should be a chief, captain or head of the group of lectors and commentators.

In some parishes practice sessions are held once a month. All those present get an opportunity to perform and have their work evaluated. Evaluation can be made by the priest, the chief lector or by comments volunteered by the other performers. Sometimes a professional speech instructor is invited to conduct a session.

Purposes, Aims, Goals

Practice sessions have long range goals and immediate ones.

Long range. Long range goals are detailed by one parish in this manner:

1. To achieve a commendable and successful Mass participation program in any parish, forceful and enthusiastic leadership on the part of lectors and commentators is essential.

2. As a commentator, you must be both an instructor and leader of the congregation. You are the first person to meet them and to form them into a worshipping community. Be prompt and precise in your introductions and comments. Speak with helpful conviction and friendly authority. Be reverent and feel the sacred importance of what you are doing.

53

3. As lector, reader of the Sacred Word, you must remember that your reading may never be a mere recitation; but a sincere and dignified presentation of the Word of God. Prepare beforehand. Note unusual words. Study the total meaning. Always read with absolute clarity, dignity, understanding and warmth, but not to the point of becoming overdramatic. Handle the book with reverence. Be neat in your appearance. To be sure that you are being heard, consult with someone in the back of the church after your performance or by pre-arrangement with someone look for a sign from him in the back of the church during the performance, such as holding his hand to his ear if you are not projecting loudly and distinctly.

4. "As leaders of God's people at prayer," remember these words from the Constitution on the Sacred Liturgy:

> "Servers, lectors, commentators . . . exercise a genuine liturgical function. They ought, therefore, to discharge their office with the sincere piety and decorum demanded by so exalted a ministry and rightly expected of them by God's people" (Article 29).

Another long range goal is improvement. In order to improve, a performer must be aware of what constitutes good performance. He sees a difference between reading aloud, oral interpretation, proclamation, communication and listener response. He judges his performance against these criteria to determine to what degree he is reaching the perfection of his sacred artistry. To be able to judge well and evaluate professionally, he develops the skill of listening carefully to himself and others. As a result of this philosophy, he learns that he must:

1. Earn the right to read through study and practice.
2. Be eager to share his material with the congregation with contagious enthusiasm and suppressed excitement.
3. Demonstrate leadership through conviction, authority, teaching and inspiration.

To achieve these ends, he experiences four stages of development. The first is just getting up there scared to death and expecting the loudspeaking system to do the work for him. Consequently, he does not even try to project his words, and even fails to enunciate properly, thinking that the public address system will magnify his murmurings to be articulate enough to be heard by the audience.

The second stage of his development is "loud and clear." With the overconfidence of the "sophomore who has been there," he blasts out his voice without modulation, shading or variety, a splendid step for beginners in rehearsal but not the accomplished ideal to be sought in actual performance.

The third stage of development is the stage of the melodramatic ham, another stage excellent for practice and rehearsal (because it pushes the performer beyond the fear barrier) but not the final goal for performance in church.

Finally, in the fourth stage the performer reaches the artistic level. His technique is unobtrusive but effective. He evokes response in the heart and mind of the listener without being "all thumbs" but with a grace, an ease and an artistry he dared not believe possible at the start. Now he takes time to be magnificent. He knows when to inflect, to stress, to shade and to enkindle divine Love with the divine Word.

Reaching this level of artistic performance requires the type of person who is willing to be prompt and on time, reliable and "there," desirous of improving, willing to take criticism, interested in Scripture, willing to study and rehearse and, most of all, in possession of the right attitude.

Immediate goals. The immediate goals of practice sessions are rehearsal techniques, acoustics, microphones, script, recording and playback, and evaluation.

1. *Rehearsal techniques.* When you, as a lector or commentator are given your assignment for the following Sunday or for a practice session, you should, first of all, accept three basic assumptions: one, no matter how talented or experienced you are, you must prepare and rehearse to be at your best; two, "reading over" is not rehearsing; three, you will accomplish more by practicing frequently for short periods of time than only once, over an extended period of time.

The first step in rehearsal is to read the passage out loud to yourself. The rendition need not be loud or interpreted, but it should be vocalized. This procedure gives you the first sense of oral proclamation. Now, try it again with some volume and projection, some stress of important words and emotional coloring. Read to yourself. Listen to yourself. You won't like part of what you hear, and that reaction is excellent. Already you are critical of your work and motivated to do better.

Try it again. Go through the melodramatic stage of development. Be creative. Try different interpretations. Push your vocal effort in several directions. If you are in doubt as to how much expression you should give to your effort, give *more* rather than *less*. This is rehearsal time. You can't hurt anyone, even yourself.

Finally, you are ready for your own private, personal dress rehearsal. Imagine yourself in front of the congregation. See the people in the pews. Feel your feet on the floor of the sanctuary. Notice a few individuals coming in late. Hear someone cough, or a baby cry. Start, read, project, interpret, proclaim, communicate, evoke response. You are on the stage of the Word of the Lord, and He wants you to perform at your best.

2. *Acoustics.* When you sit in certain spots of a church, and you hear echoes and echoes of echoes and sound distortions and dead spots, you say the acoustics are bad. The nature of the church in its physical construction and materials frequently causes the performer difficulty in being heard and understood easily in all areas of the church. No matter what the acoustical problem may be, it becomes the performer's function to adjust to it. The following techniques are helpful:

    a. Experiment with the proper mixture of treble and bass in the sound system. Too much treble accentuates the higher frequencies. Too much bass produces an "FM sound," smooth, low and frequently indistinct and seemingly inarticulate. Trained professional baritone voices can "get away with" more bass in the sound system. The average lay performer in church, however, will be more distinct and audible if the treble is slightly increased.

    b. Slow down your rate.

    c. Use smaller phrases.

       Pause more frequently if only slightly.

    d. Enunciate carefully. Prolong the accented vowel sounds. Make the consonant sounds accurately and crisply.

    e. Try different mixtures of the four elements of sound: force, range, quality, and pacing. Let someone check up on your performance from several spots in the church.

    f. Remember that the acoustical problem decreases when the pews are full of people. Echoes and distortions are cut down, but the sad fact remains that they are seldom completely eliminated.

3. *Microphones.* Proper use of the microphone is important for many reasons but especially because of the deterioration in hearing that occurs as people grow older.

The ability to understand what is being said depends to a large extent on recognition of the consonant sounds in speech. These consonants relate to the higher frequencies near 2000 cycles and up. These are the frequencies that impart intelligibility.

The United States Public Health Service reports that average hearing discloses:

    a. The young (10 to 19 years of age) show no deterioration

    b. Older persons (30-39 years of age) begin to show critical impairment in the 3520 cycle area

    c. Much older persons (50-59) show marked deterioration

    d. The deterioration is worse in men than in women.

Frequently the listener *tells* the performer that he is not being understood. A lifting of the head or tilting of it, a leaning forward or cupping of the hand next to the ear are the more obvious signs. The seasoned performer detects these signs at a glance and makes immediate vocal adjustments.

More than thirty different types of microphones are available for every religious ceremonial requirement from small lavaliers to floor-standing dynamic or condenser microphones.

The most popular public address microphones are the dynamic and the condenser. The condenser is similar to the dynamic microphone in that it uses a diaphragm, but differs from it in that the diaphragm does not activate a coiled wire but, instead, has an electrode as a back plate. This technical material is inserted here only to impress you with the fact that you must not get too close to a microphone when speaking because sounds such as P, T, K, F, TH, S, and CH will produce a sharpened, sputtering, irritating consonant effect. To avoid this effect, lower the microphone to shoulder level and speak into it from a distance of one to two feet away. How close or how far away you work depends upon how much you project and how much volume you use. A mathematical principle is involved in mike distance and volume: if you double your distance from the mike, you lose one half of your volume. In other words, if your volume is 100 at 2 feet, your volume will be 50 at 4 feet. If, therefore, you want to back away from a mike that is set for a certain volume, you must project your voice more. It is well to have a practice session with the equipment which your parish church uses.

Another problem to watch for in the use of a microphone is staying on the beam. As a performer, you should not turn too much to either side. Ideally each ambo should have two microphones, one to the left, and one to the right. When there is one mike only, do not turn to the side unless you step back slightly first. Then, you may turn a bit, and, if you do, be sure to project.

4. *The Script.* In some parishes the congregation does not get a copy of the readings, but, rather, is asked to listen to the lector. In those parishes, however, where the congregation does follow the readings from a missalette, the lector should use the same translation the people use. If he uses a reading from the Jerusalem Bible while the people follow from the New American Bible, communication is upset and frustrated.

For some readers the missalette print is too small. If this is your predicament, type the readings in triple space. In addition, follow these mechanical aids:

1. Underline with a straight *horizontal* line the idea-words you want to stress.

2. Underline with a *wavy* line the feeling-words you want to make vivid.

3. Draw vertical lines | for phrasing | and pausing.

The Practice Session

These mechanical aids of script mark-up are of great help in preparation, rehearsal and performance. Take the following sentence, for example and analyze it:

> We know what we are
> But we know not
> What we may be.

What words would you stress? On the basis of your analysis, read the sentence aloud. Ask someone else to do the same. Compare notes. Any disagreement?

As another example, take the dialogue between Satan and Christ (Matt. 4, 8-10):

> Satan: All these I will bestow on you
> if you prostrate yourself in
> homage before me.
>
> Jesus: Away with you, Satan! Scripture
> has it: you shall do homage to
> the Lord your God. Him alone
> shall you adore!

The usual interpretation given to Jesus' words is found in these underlined words: You shall do homage to the *Lord* your *God*. Him *alone* shall you adore. Now try another interpretation: *You* shall do homage to the Lord your God. Him alone shall *you* adore.

Does this interpretation make clearer and more forceful who the person is who should do the adoring?

As a general rule, we should try to stress words which by their very nature are the important words. The parts of speech in the order of their importance are:

> Verbs
> Nouns
> Pronouns
> Adjectives
> Adverbs
> Prepositions

If anything at all becomes clear from this list, it is this rule:

don't be a pronoun puncher unless you have a very good reason. Even in the Gettysburg address the best authorities state that Lincoln said "government of the *people,* by the *people,* for the *people,* and not *of, by for.*

As one last addendum, placed here because the writer could think of no better place to put it, let the reader be aware that he should be ready to turn the page before he gets to the last word of that page.

5. *Recordings and Playback.* Imagine a seventeen-year old savage looking into a mirror for the first time. Can't you hear him asking, "Do I look like that?" Something similar happens when individuals tape their presentations for the first time. Frequently, while listening to the playback, they ask, "Do I sound like that?" Sometimes they question the accuracy of the recording equipment.

The conflict lies, of course, in what we are and what we'd like to be, and few of us are satisfied with what we are. In fact, one voice instructor says, "I can usually tell whose voice we're listening to in the playback just by looking around the room. It's usually the voice of someone who looks embarrassed."

This embarrassment is natural. When you listen to a playback of your voice, you hear it differently from the way you speak. When you speak, you hear two kinds of vibrations: those inside your head and those outside your head. When you listen to a playback of your voice, you hear only those vibrations outside your head, the same vibrations others hear when they listen to you speak.

Another reason for embarrassment is familiarity. You are so familiar with the sound of your voice that most of the time you pay little attention to how you sound. Suddenly in the playback, your voice is set apart from you. You hear yourself as others hear you. You are like the savage looking into the mirror for the first time and you don't want to believe what you see or hear.

The video television tape is more believeable than the audio-radio tape because we tend to believe what we can see more than what we hear only. There's no denying what we did visually on the video tape, and with our acceptance of the visual and the breaking down of our pride, we tend to believe a little more also how we sound. But this is not the end.

Playing back a tape once does little good. The person who is taped does not believe all he sees and hears the first time he sees and hears it. He needs to hear and see it several times before he is able to objectify the entire package of visual, vocal and verbal stimuli.

Two questions might be asked at this point: Is it helpful to tape someone during the Liturgy and play it back at the next meeting of the lectors? Is it helpful to tape someone when he does not know he is being taped? The answer to both of these questions is a definite, "Yes." Any technique that can help us "see ourselves as others see us" promotes less delusion and more objectivity. This objectivity can be achieved by playing the tape back several times until we see ourselves as others see us.

6. *Evaluation.* Practice and experience *alone* do not make perfect. Like the yearly physical check-up, an occasional evaluation of the performer's work is most helpful.

The professional evaluator should not limit himself to what he hears the first time. He should point out, of course, what the performer did well, wherein he can improve, and then have him do a part of the selection again and again, each time working on some specific aspect whether it is stress, conversational style, tone-color, pace and pause, eye-contact, empathy or whatever. After the performer has been given a good analysis, after he has been alerted to specific avenues for improvement, after he has had a "second chance," only then, should the evaluator give the performer the final diagnosis.

In a nutshell, a man will profit from the evaluation of others if the evaluator knows what he is doing, if the performer will be humble enough to listen, and if objective truth prevails over subjective emotionalism.

And finally, beware of praise from your mother. If you're in doubt, ask your wife. Wives have an uncanny insight into truth concerning their husbands. If you're still in doubt, consult the following analysis sheet. If you can answer "yes" to questions 1-14, you can answer "a" to question 15.

AN EVALUATION CHART FOR THE LECTOR AND COMMENTATOR

1. Does he give evidence of preparation and rehearsal?
2. Is his appearance appropriate?
3. Is his bodily response alert?
4. Are there any distracting mannerisms?
5. Is his voice loud enough?
6. Does he stress the right words?
7. Does he pause in the right places?
8. Does he *talk to* rather than *read* or *recite?*
9. Does he get his voice *out* and front-forward?
10. Does he have variety in tone-color?
11. Does he use careful, crisp enunciation?
12. Does he use a change of pace?
13. Is his pronunciation correct and acceptable?
14. In summary, does he understand his material, communicate it and evoke a response in the listener?
15. In comparison to the lectors you have listened to, where would you place him?
    - a. Outstanding
    - b. Above average
    - c. Average
    - d. Below average

GENERAL BIBLIOGRAPHY

1. Aggertt, Otis J. and Elbert R. Bowen. *Communicative Reading.* New York: The Macmillan Co. Third Edition. 1972
2. Anderson, Virgil A. *Training the Speaking Voice.* New York: Oxford University Press. Second Edition. 1961
3. Bacon, Wallace A. *The Art of Interpretation.* New York: Holt, Rinehart and Winston, Inc. Second Edition. 1972
4. Bahn, Eugene and Margaret L. Bahn. *A History of Oral Interpretation.* Minneapolis: Burgess Publishing Co. 1970
5. Black, John W. and Ruth B. Irwin. *Voice and Diction.* Columbus, Ohio: Charles E. Merrill Publishing Co. 1969
6. Brack, Harold A. *Effective Oral Interpretation for Religious Leaders.* Englewood Cliffs, N. J.: Prentice-Hall, Inc. 1964
7. Brooks, Keith, Eugene Bahn and L. Lamont Okey. *The Communicative Act of Oral Interpretation.* Boston: Allyn and Bacon. 1967
8. Fisher, Hilda B. *Improving Voice and Articulation.* Boston: Houghton Mifflin Co. 1966
9. Hahn, Elise, Donald Hargis, Charles Lomas, and Daniel Vandraegen. *Basic Voice Training for Speech.* New York: McGraw-Hill Book Co., Inc. 1957
10. Hyde, Stuart W. *Television and Radio Announcing.* Boston: The Riverside Press Cambridge. 1959
11. Lamers, William M. and Joseph Staudacher. *The Speech Arts.* Chicago: Lyons and Carnahan. 1966
12. Lee, Charlotte I. *Oral Interpretation.* New York: Houghton-Mifflin Co. Fourth Edition. 1971
13. Scrivner, Louise M. *A Guide To Oral Interpretation.* New York: Odyssey Press, Inc. 1968
14. Staudacher, Joseph and Milton Bierbaum. *Business and Professional Speaking.* Milwaukee: Marquette University Bookstore. 1967

SPECIFIC BIBLIOGRAPHY

1. Celebrating Liturgy, Liturgy Training Program, Archdiocese of Chicago, 5947 N. Manton Avenue Chicago, Illinois 60646
2. Celebration, A creative Workshop Service, P.O. Box 281, Kansas City, Missouri 64141
3. Commentaries, Liturgical Commission, Diocese of Lansing, 300 W. Ottawa Street Lansing, Michigan 48933
4. Commentary on the Sunday Lectionary, Liturgical Press, Collegeville, Minnesota
5. McKenzie, John S.J. Dictionary of the Bible, Milwaukee: Bruce Publishing Co. 1965
6. Proclamation, A Commentary, Liturgical Commission, 320 Cathedral St., Baltimore, Maryland 21201
7. Reading the Word of God, United States Catholic Conference, 1312 Massachusetts Ave. N.W., Washington, D.C. 20005
8. Read the Word of the Lord, Delaney Publications, 720 N. Rush St., Chicago, Illinois 60611